Dearest

Valentine's Day Coloring Book

Ayn Eliot

Happy Coloring

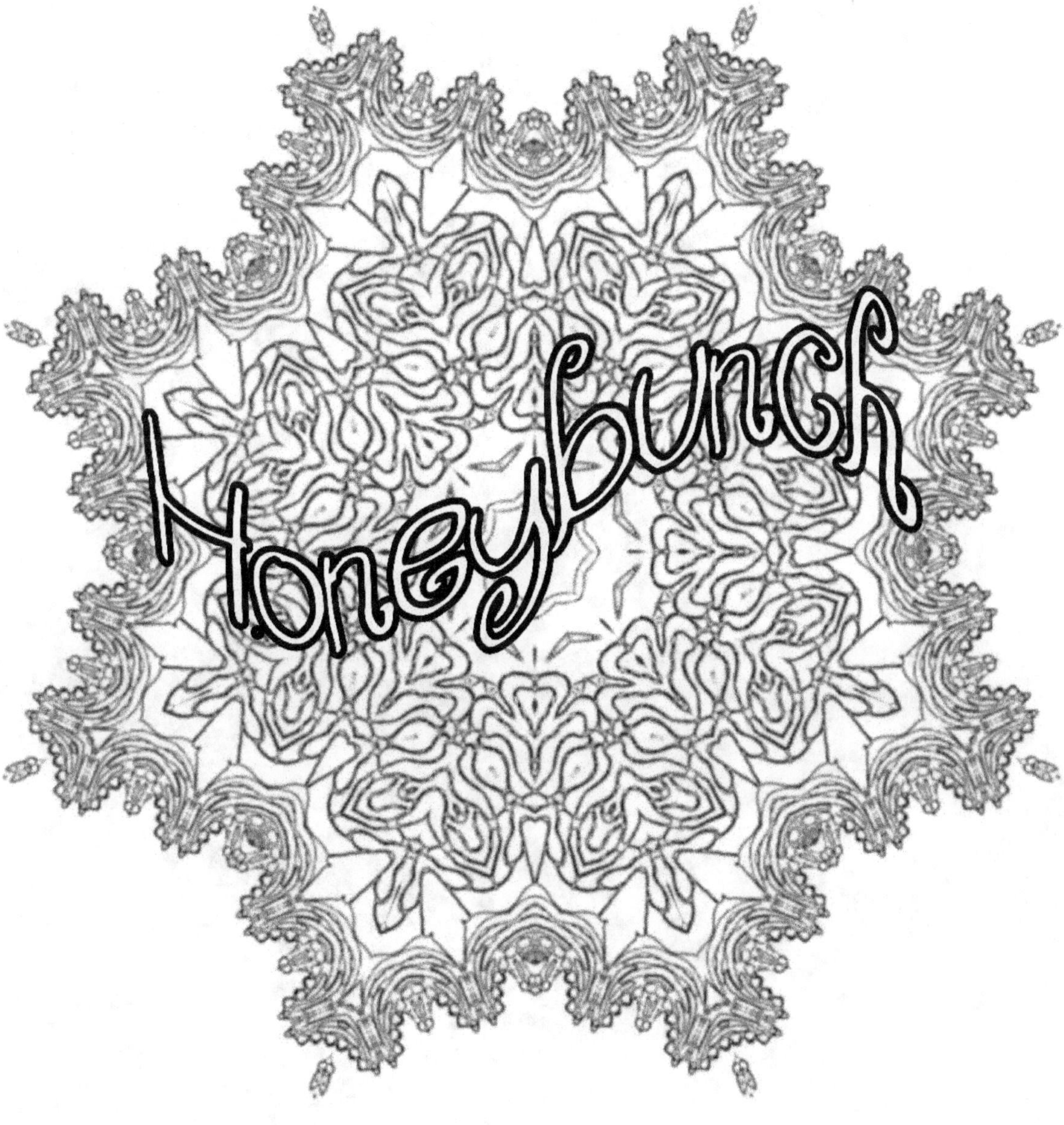
Honeybunch

My Beloved One

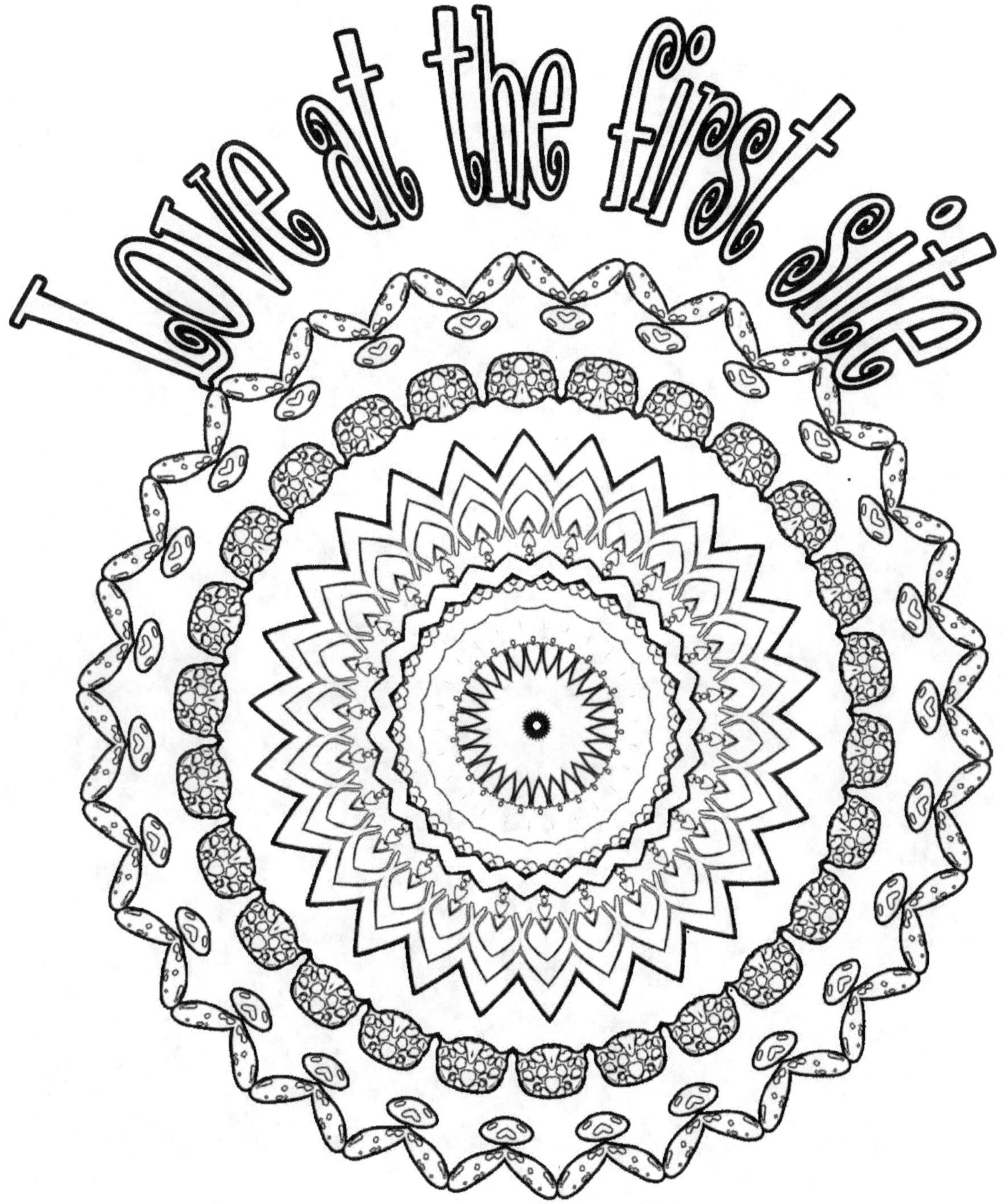
Love at the first site

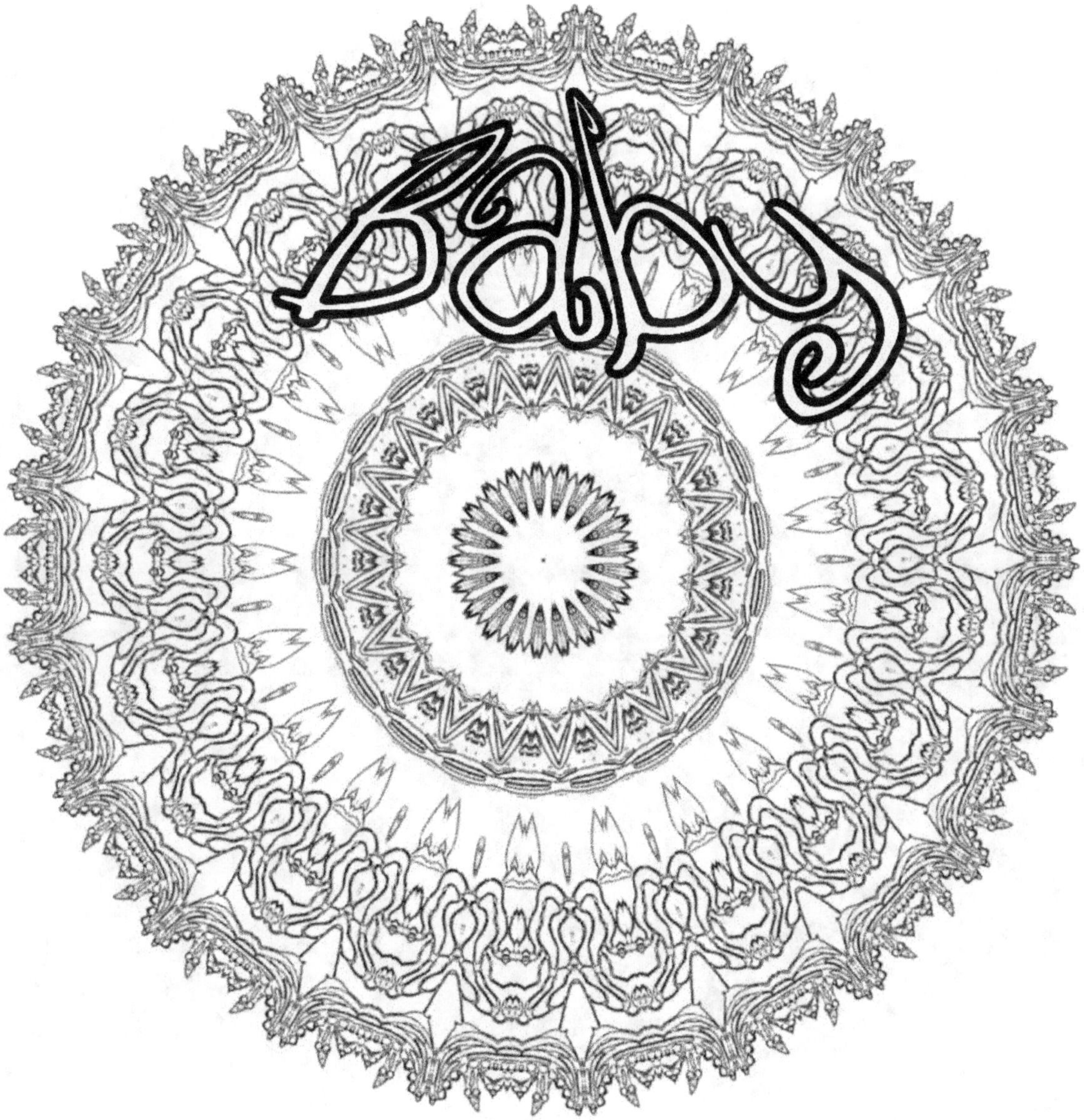
Baby

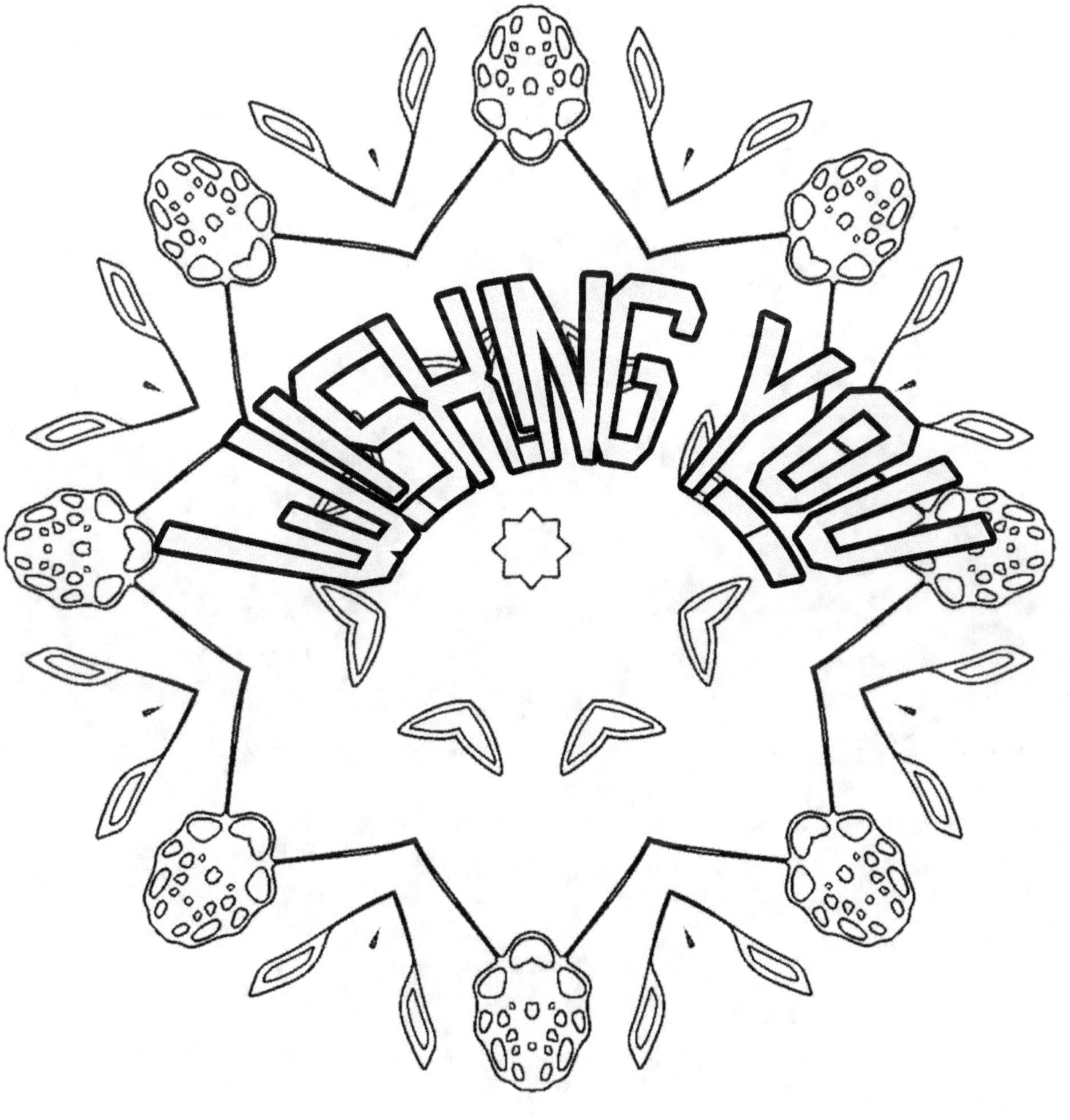
WISHING YOU

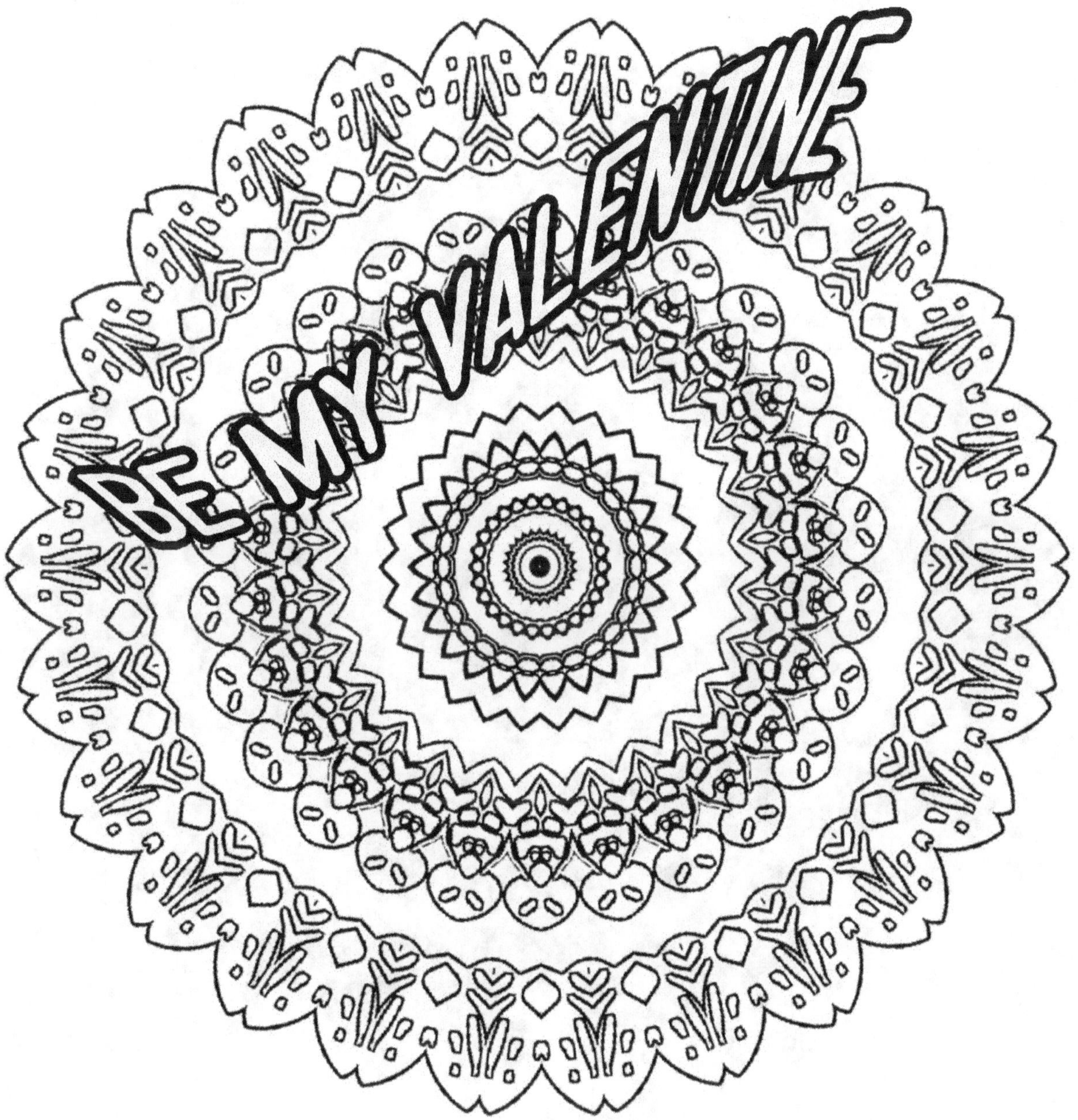
BE MY VALENITNE

A Cup Of Love

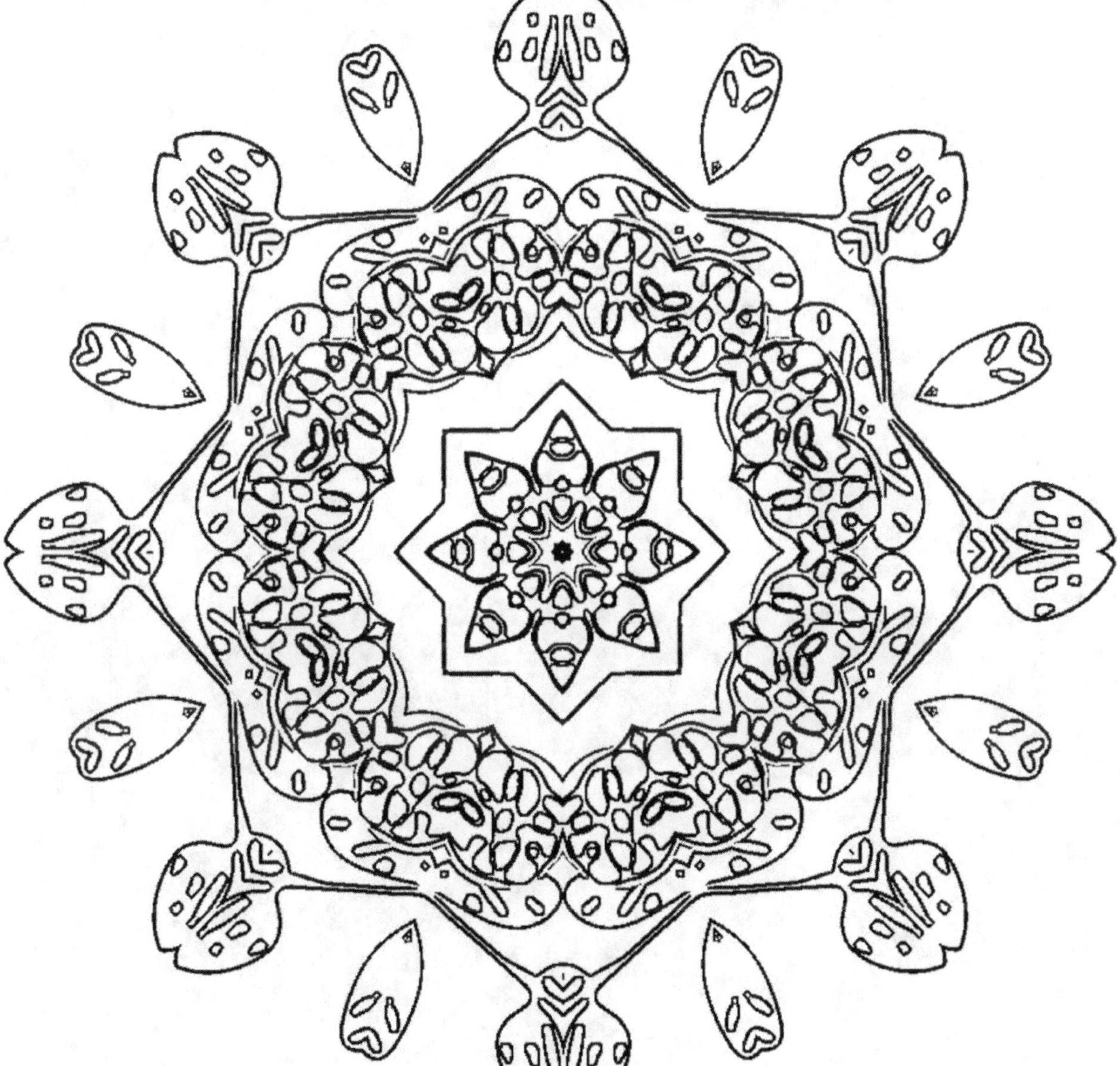

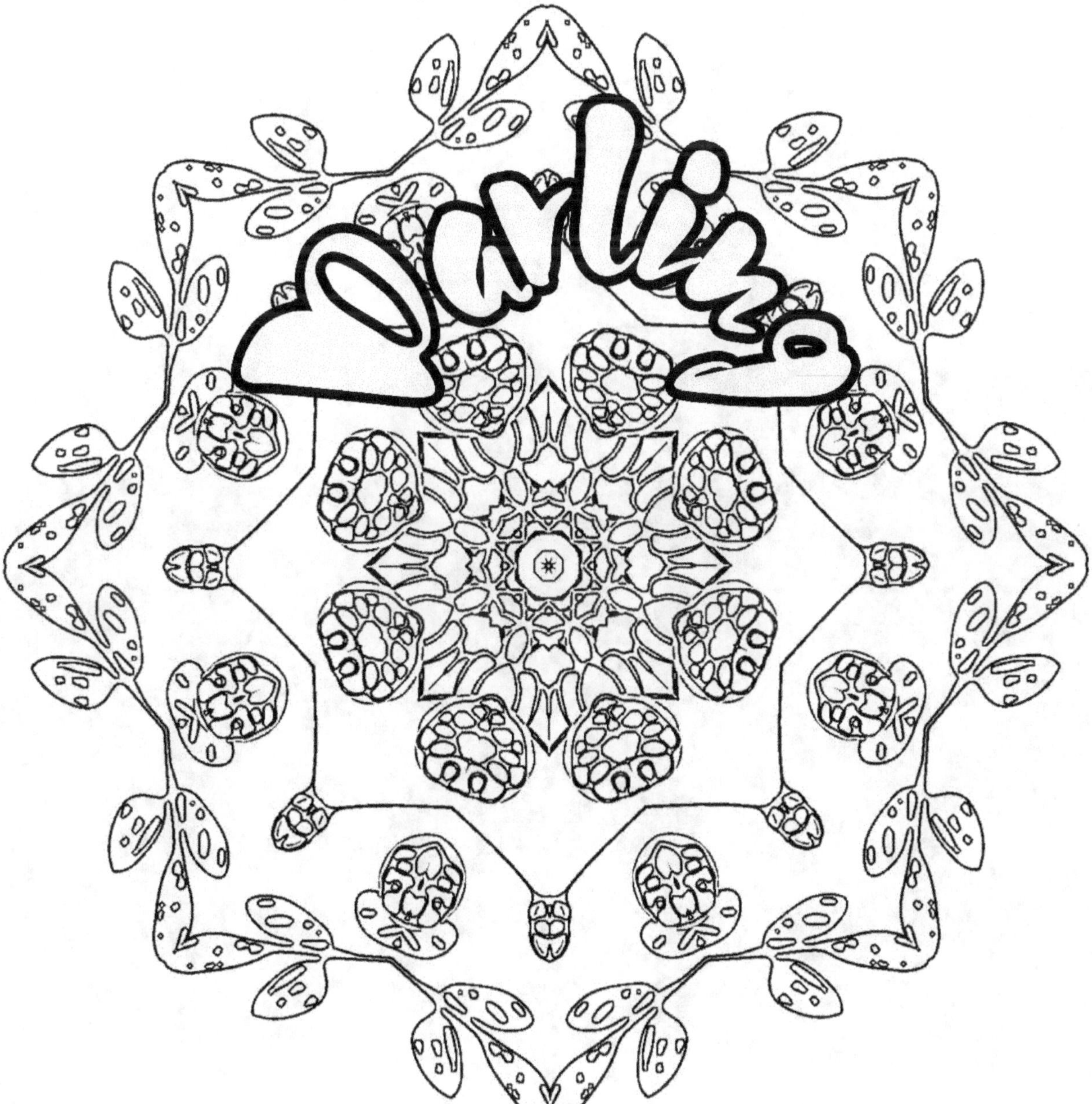
Darling

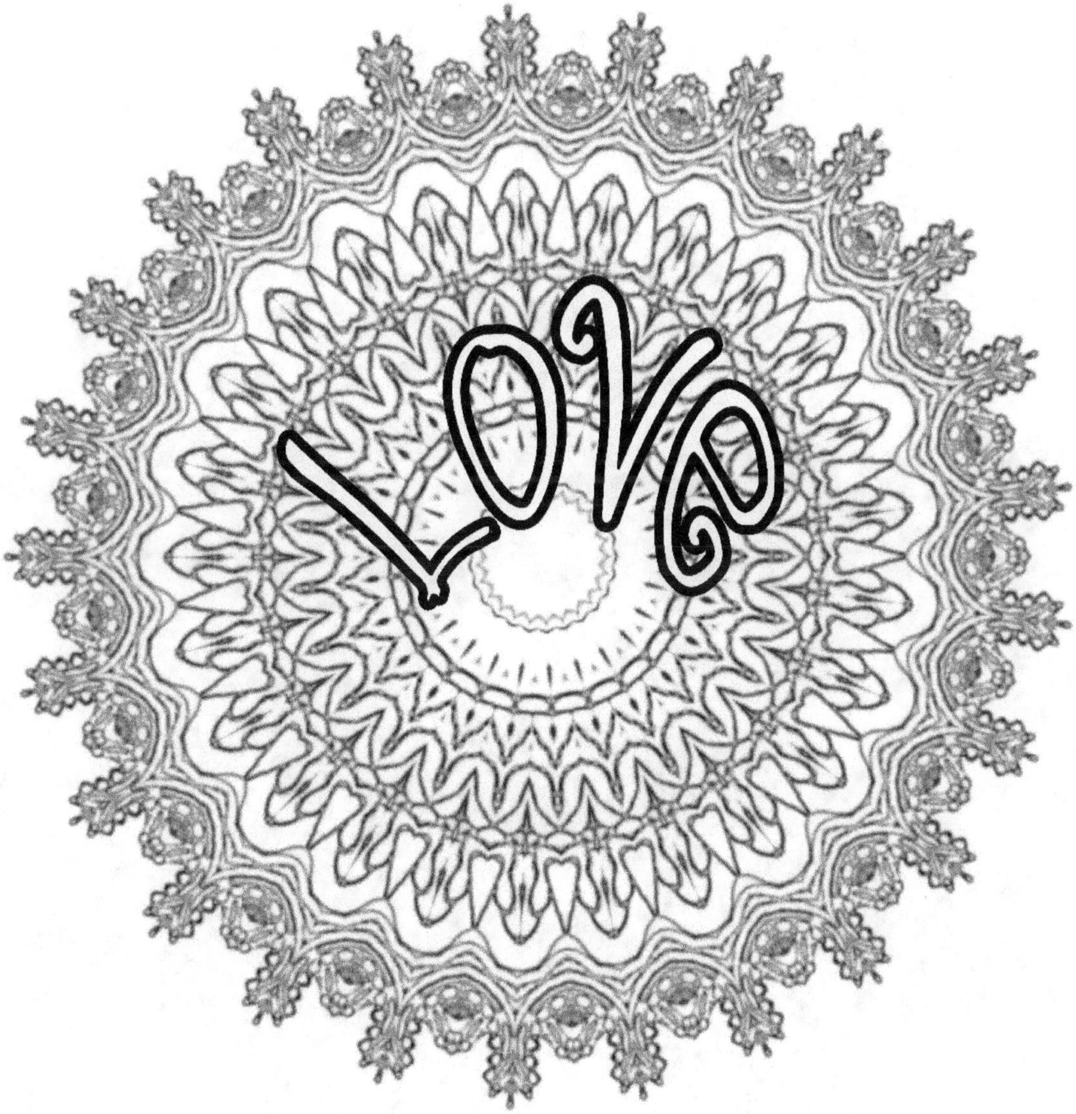
Love

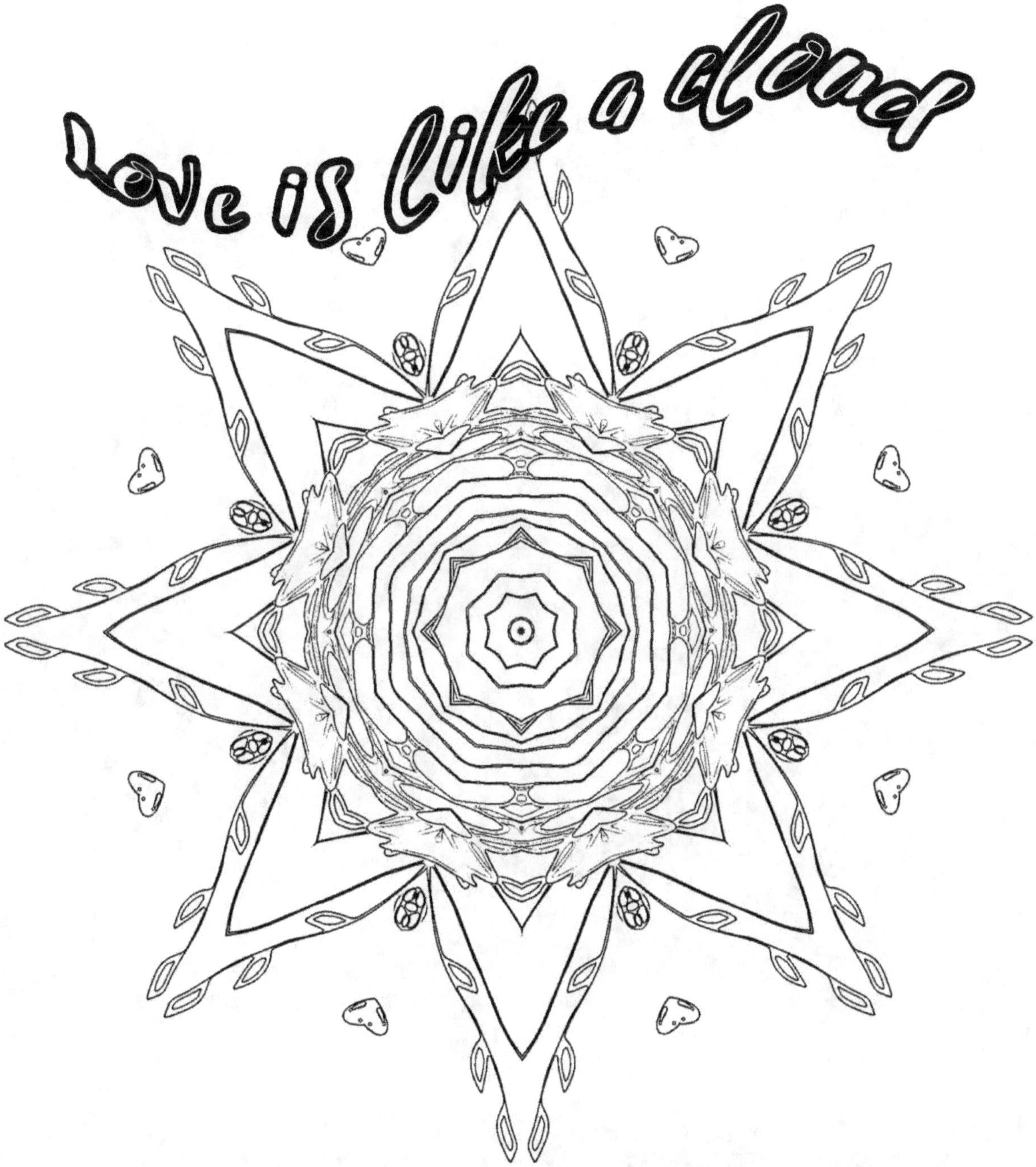
Love is like a cloud

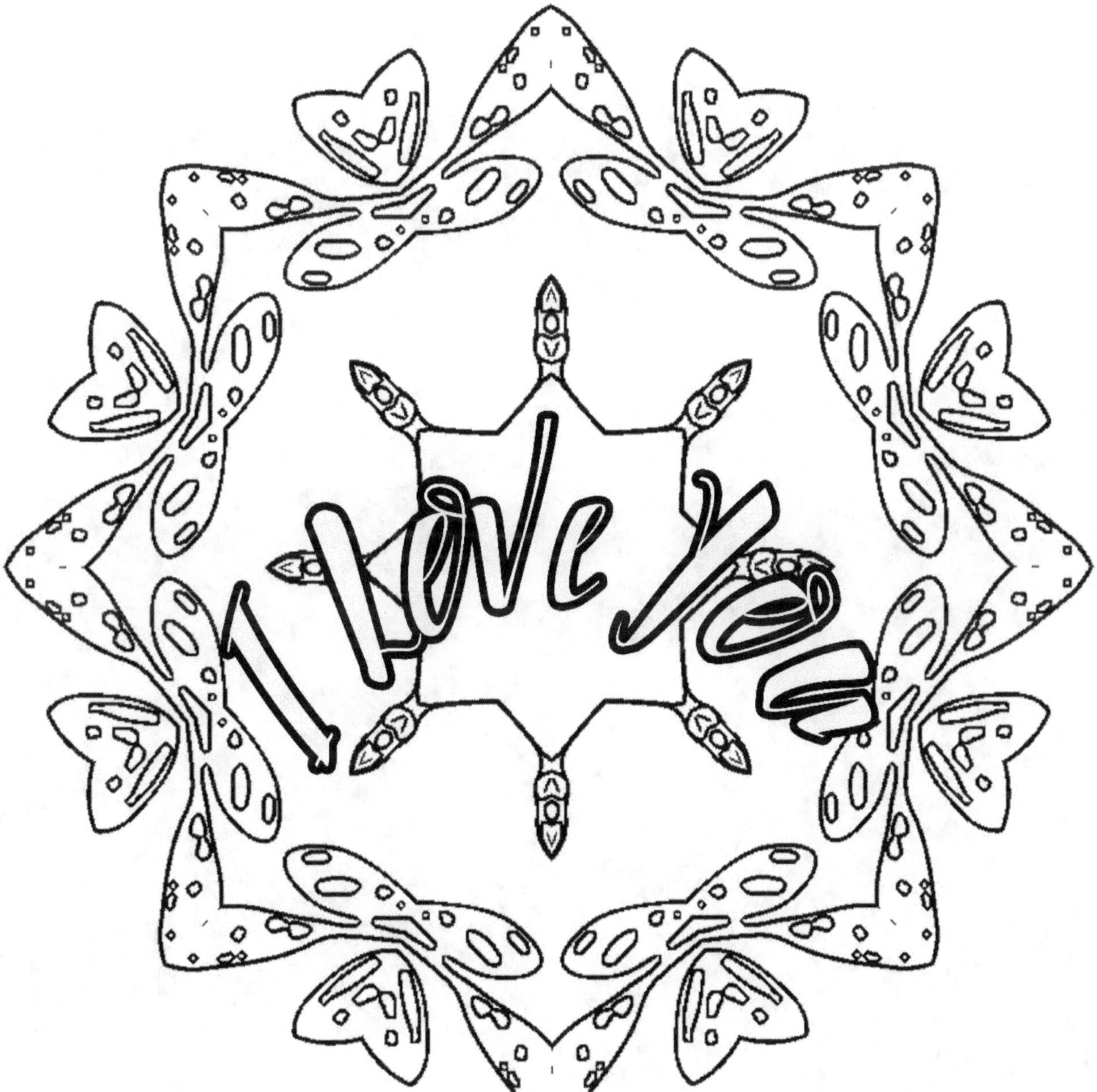
I Love You

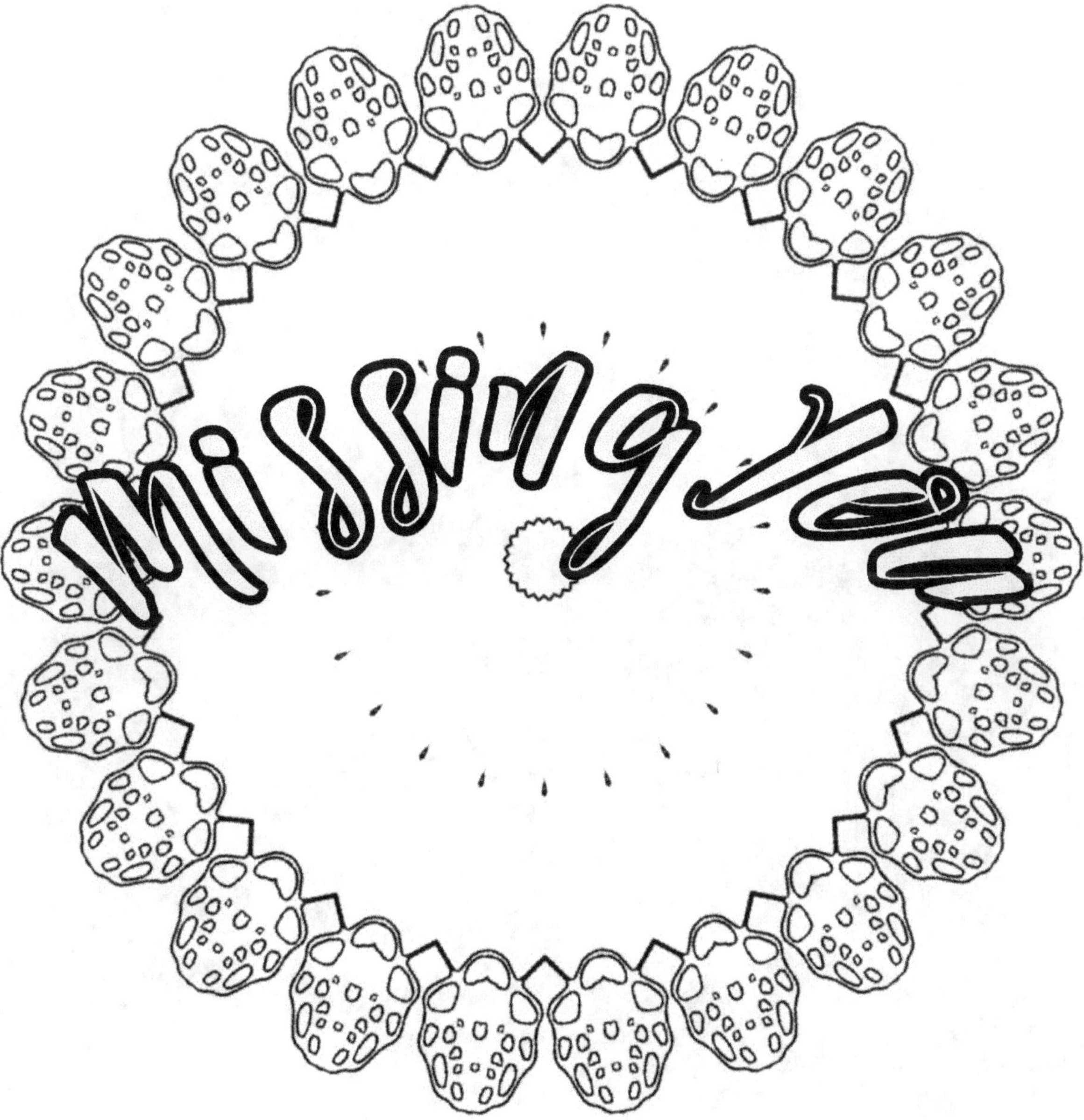
Missing You

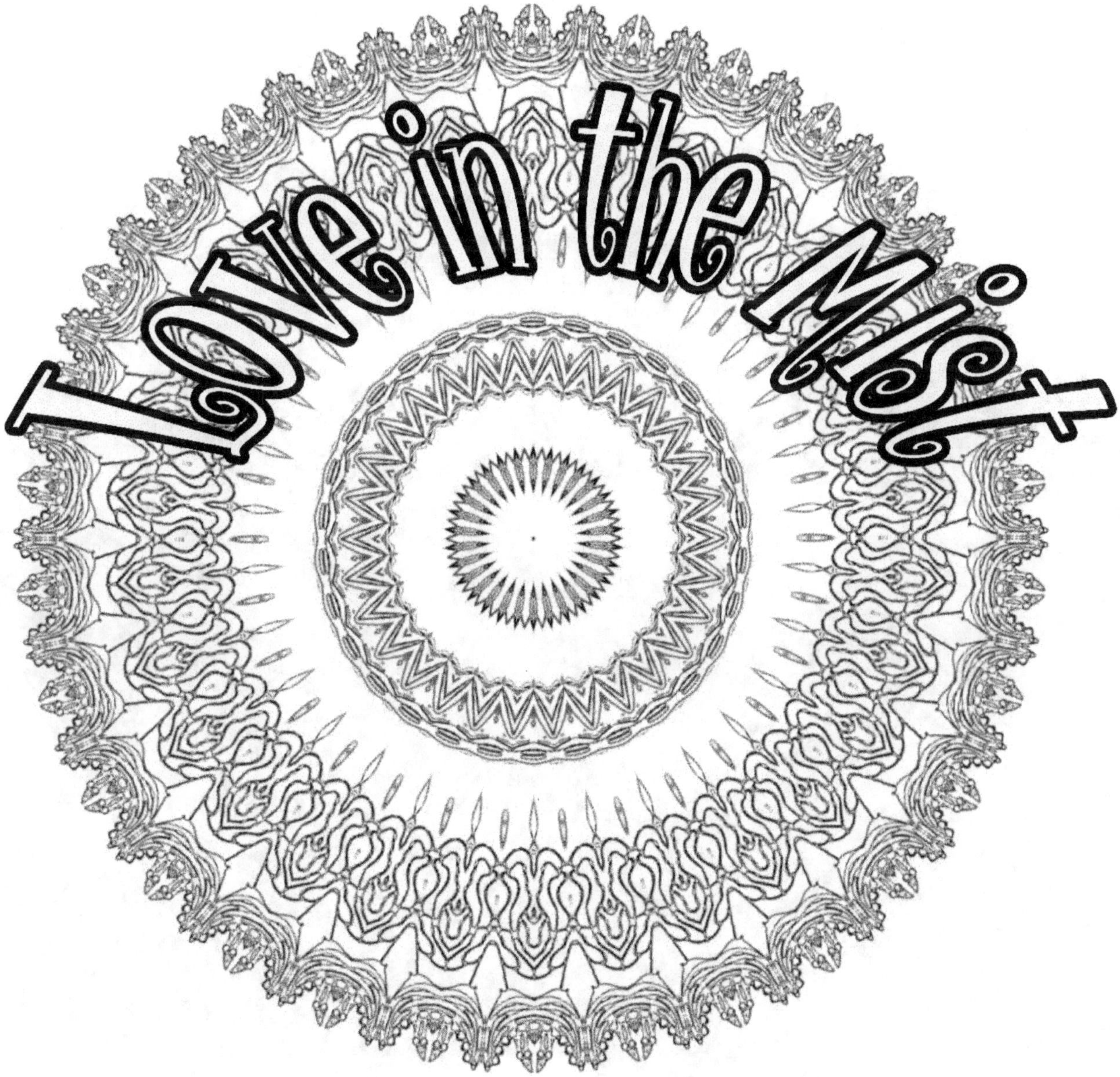
Love in the Mist

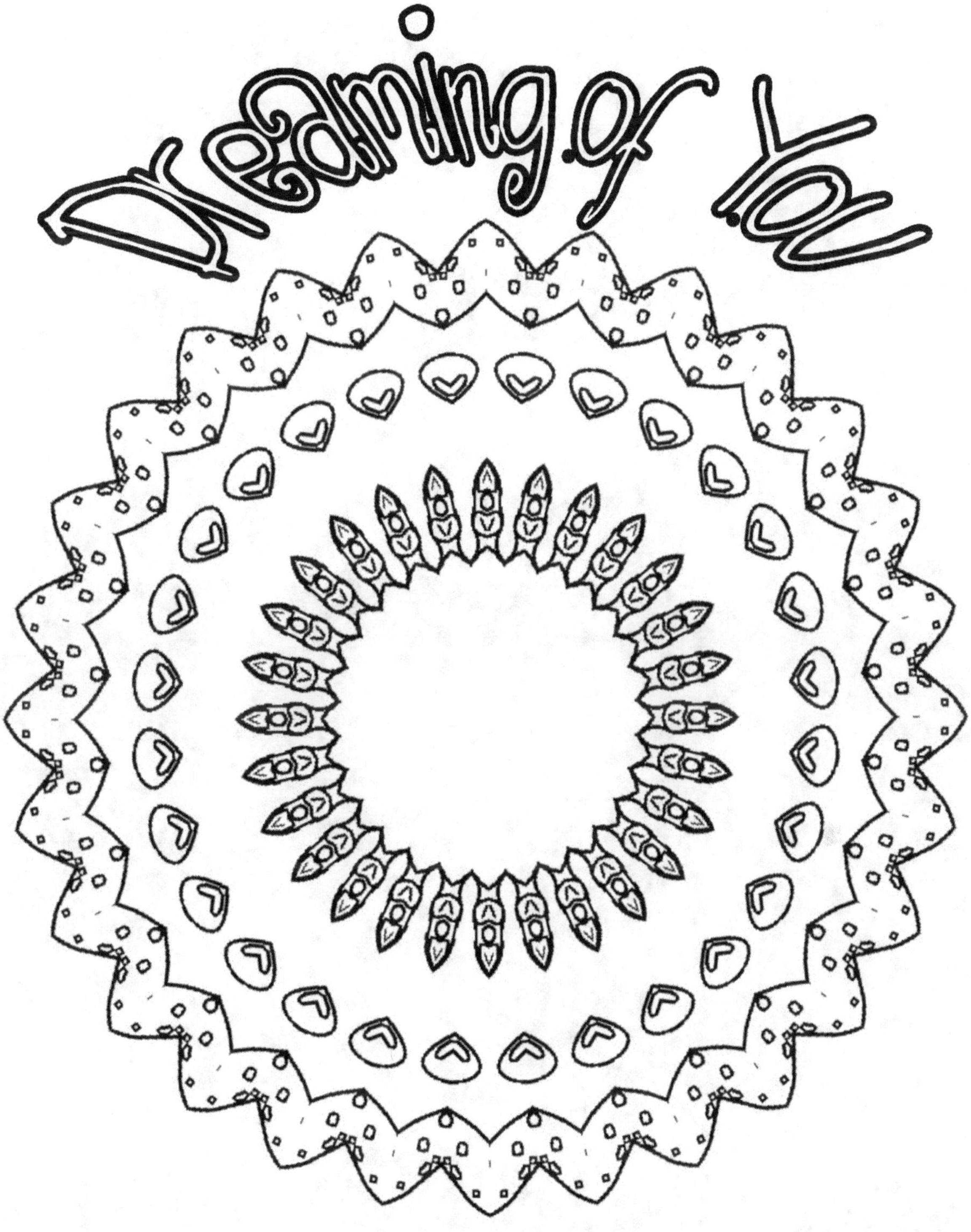
Dreaming of You

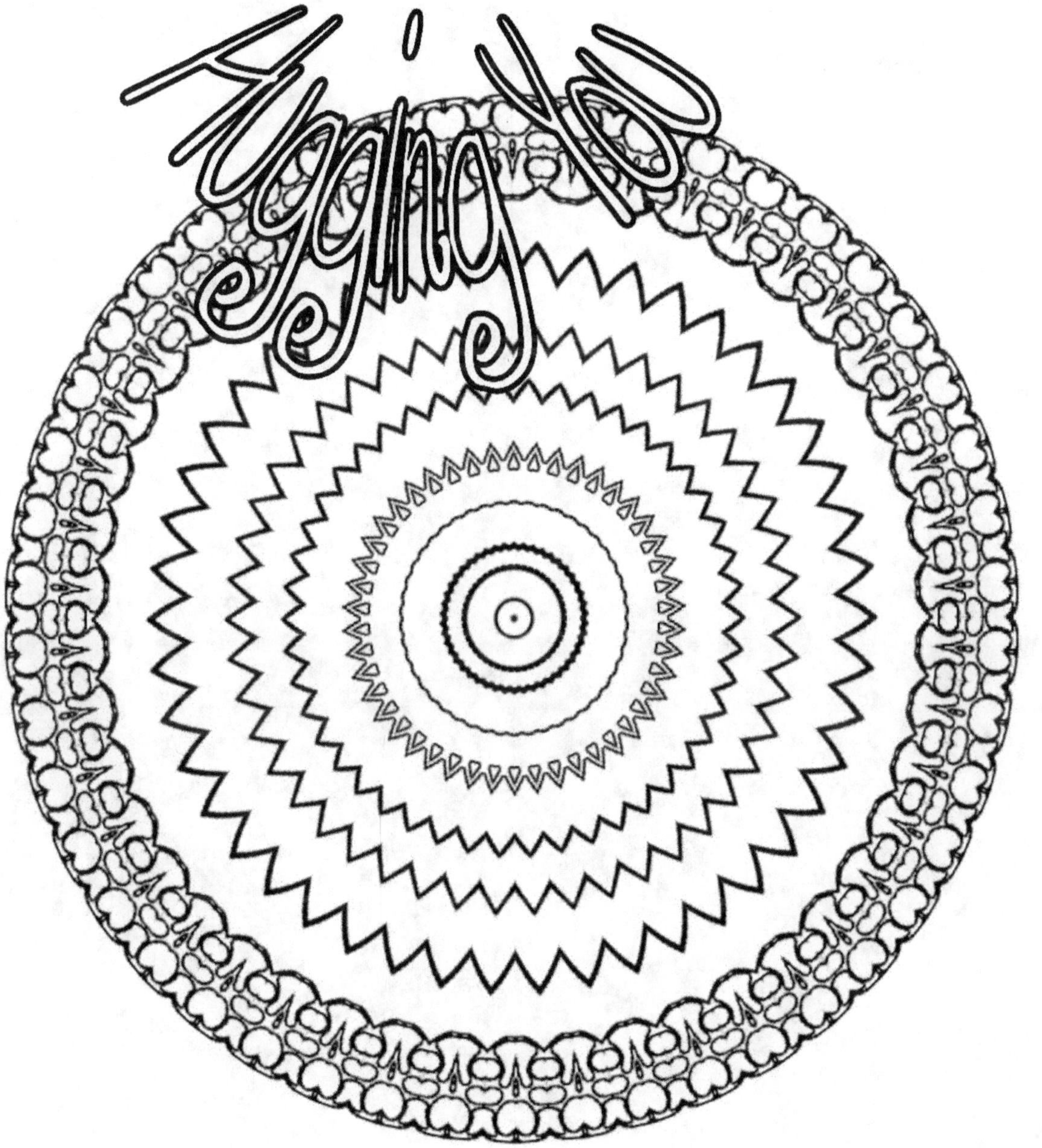
Hugging You

SWEETHEART

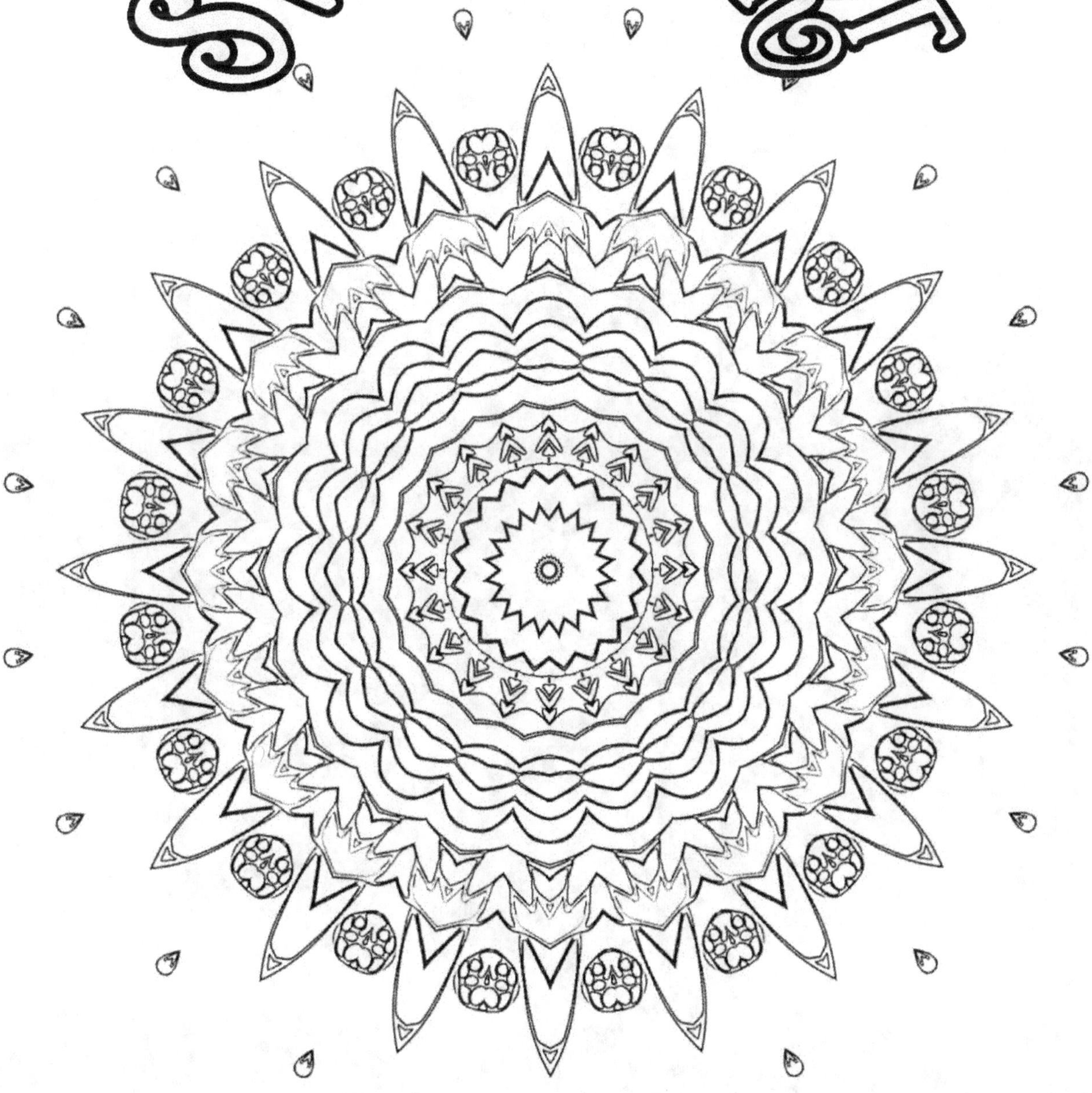

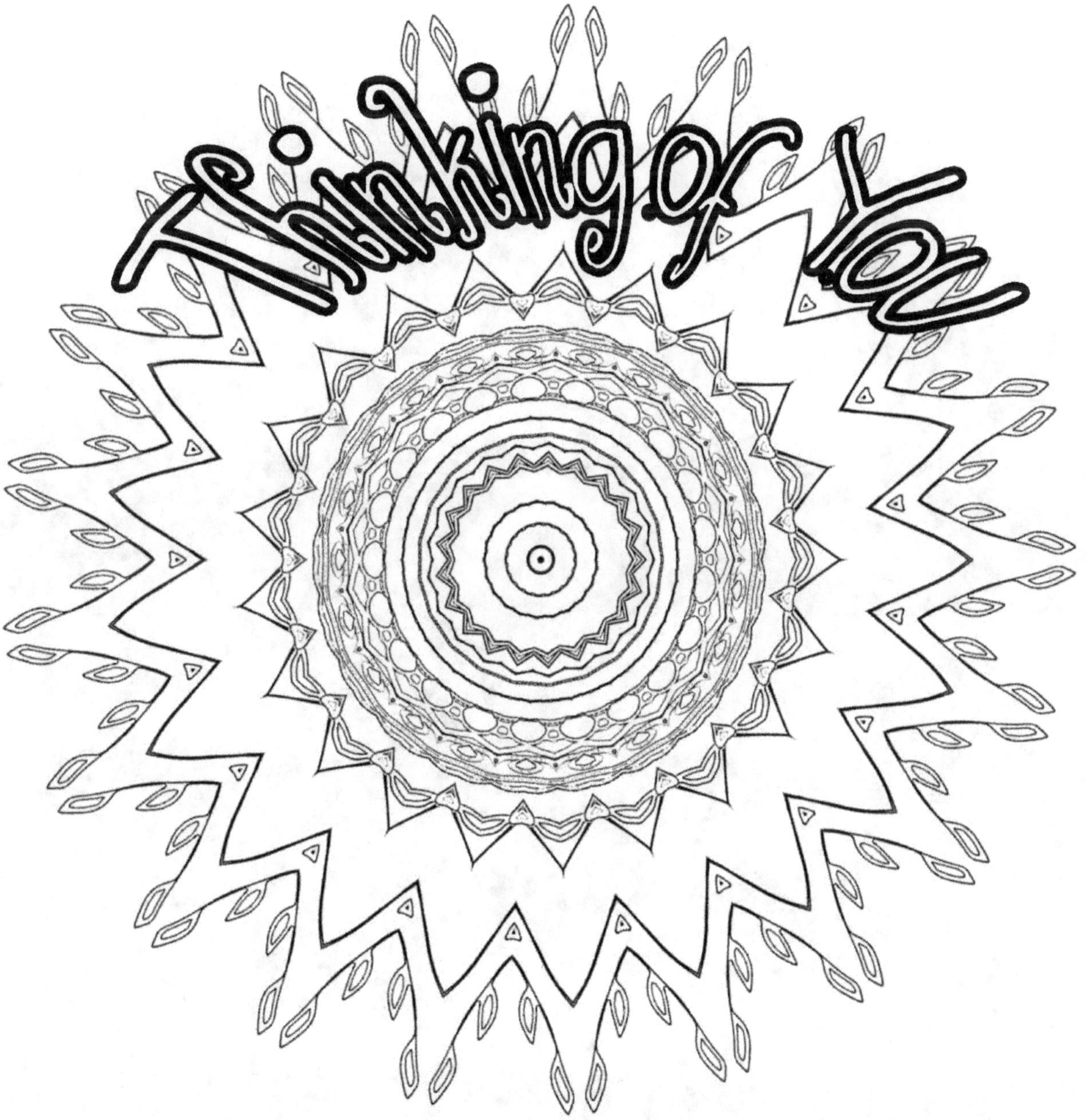
Thinking of You

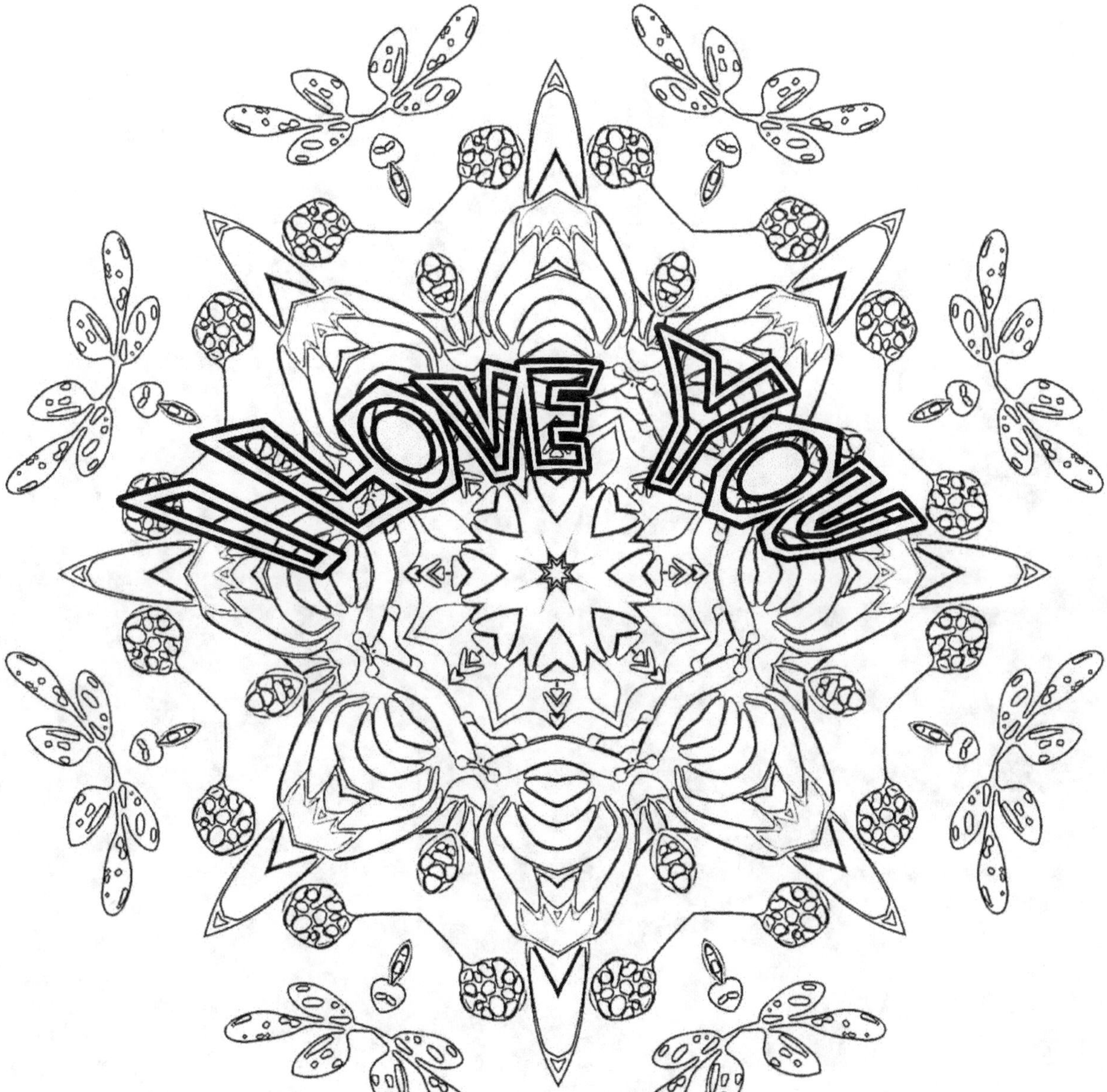
I LOVE YOU

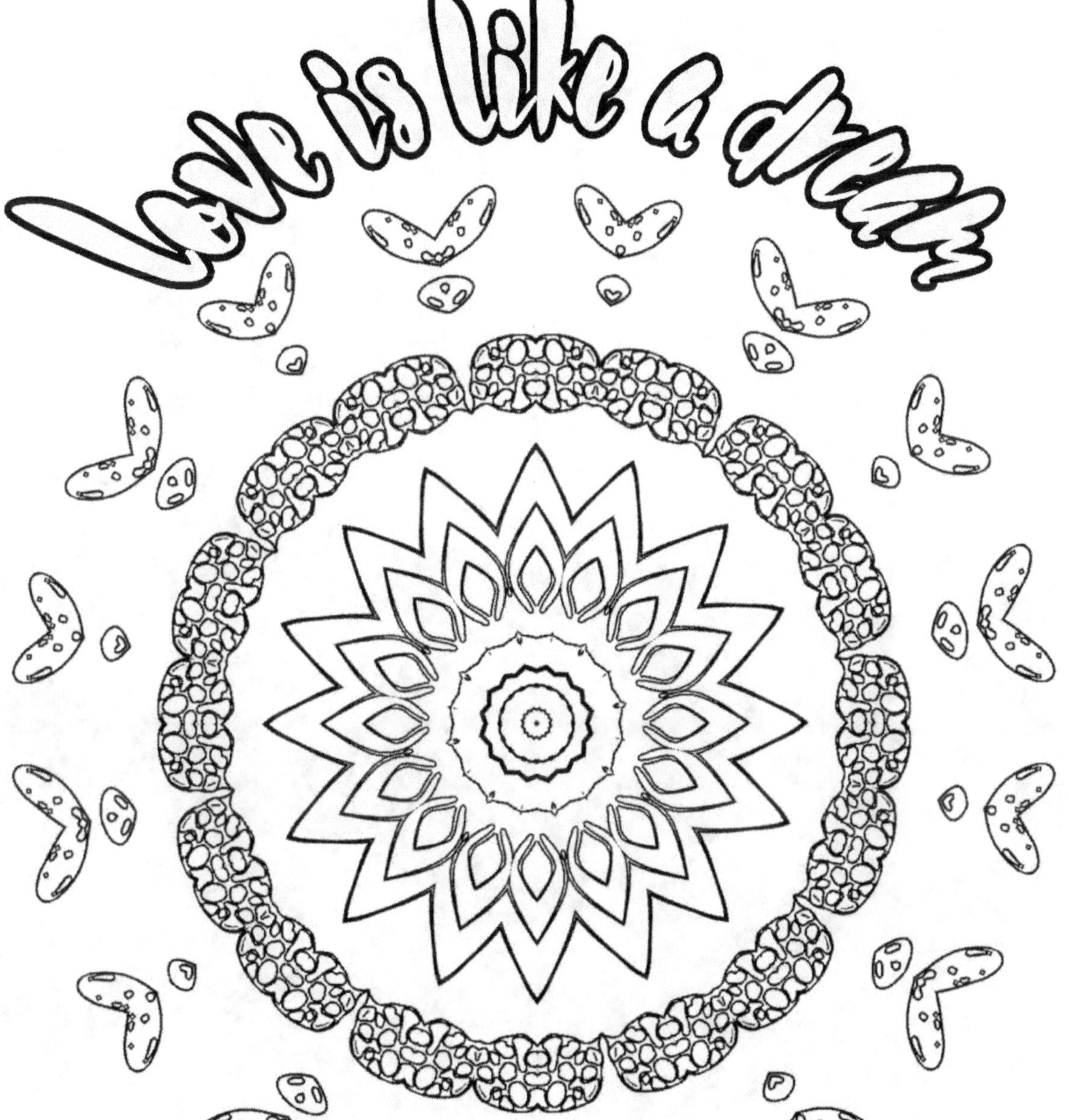
love is like a dream

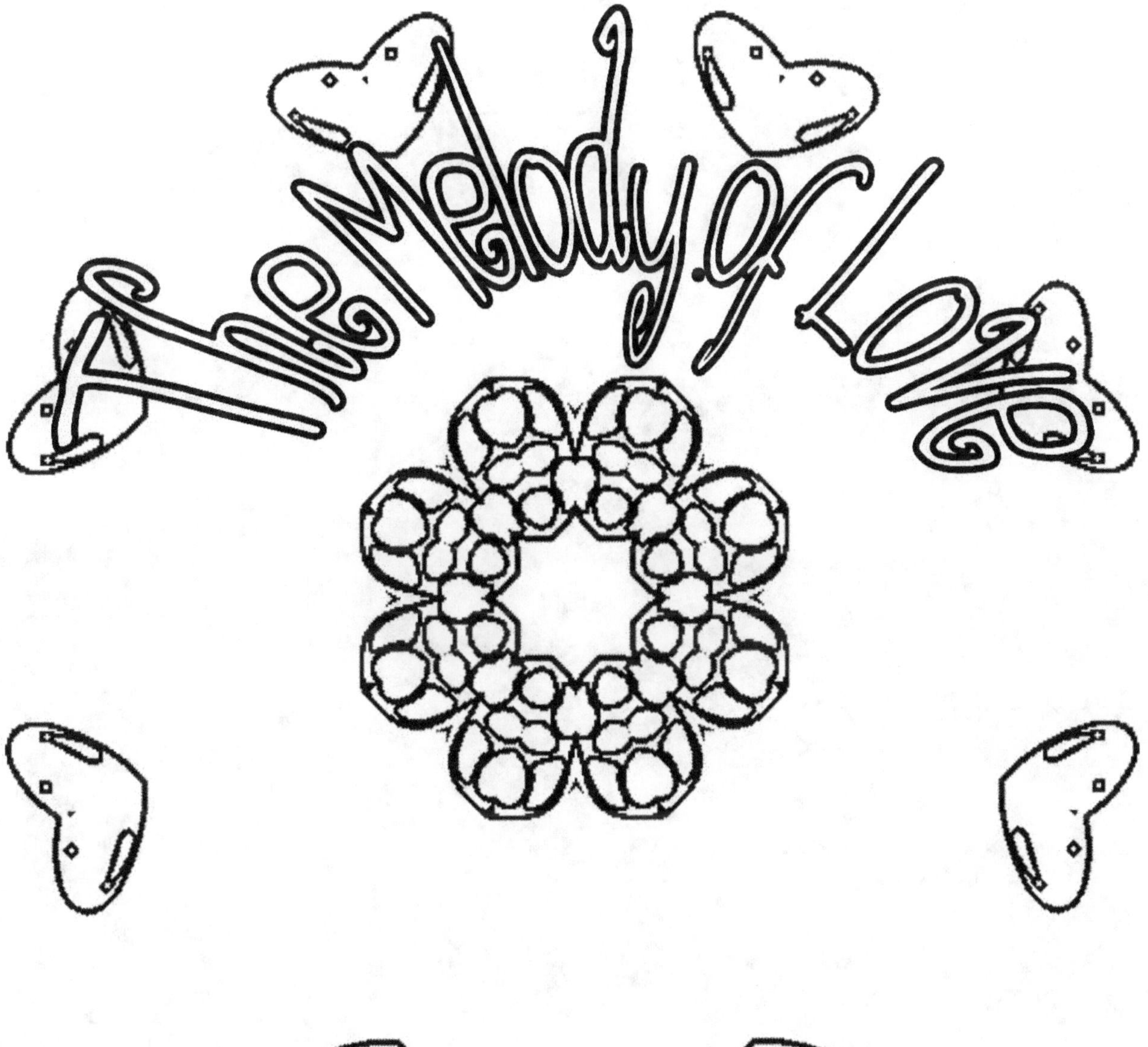
The Melody of Love

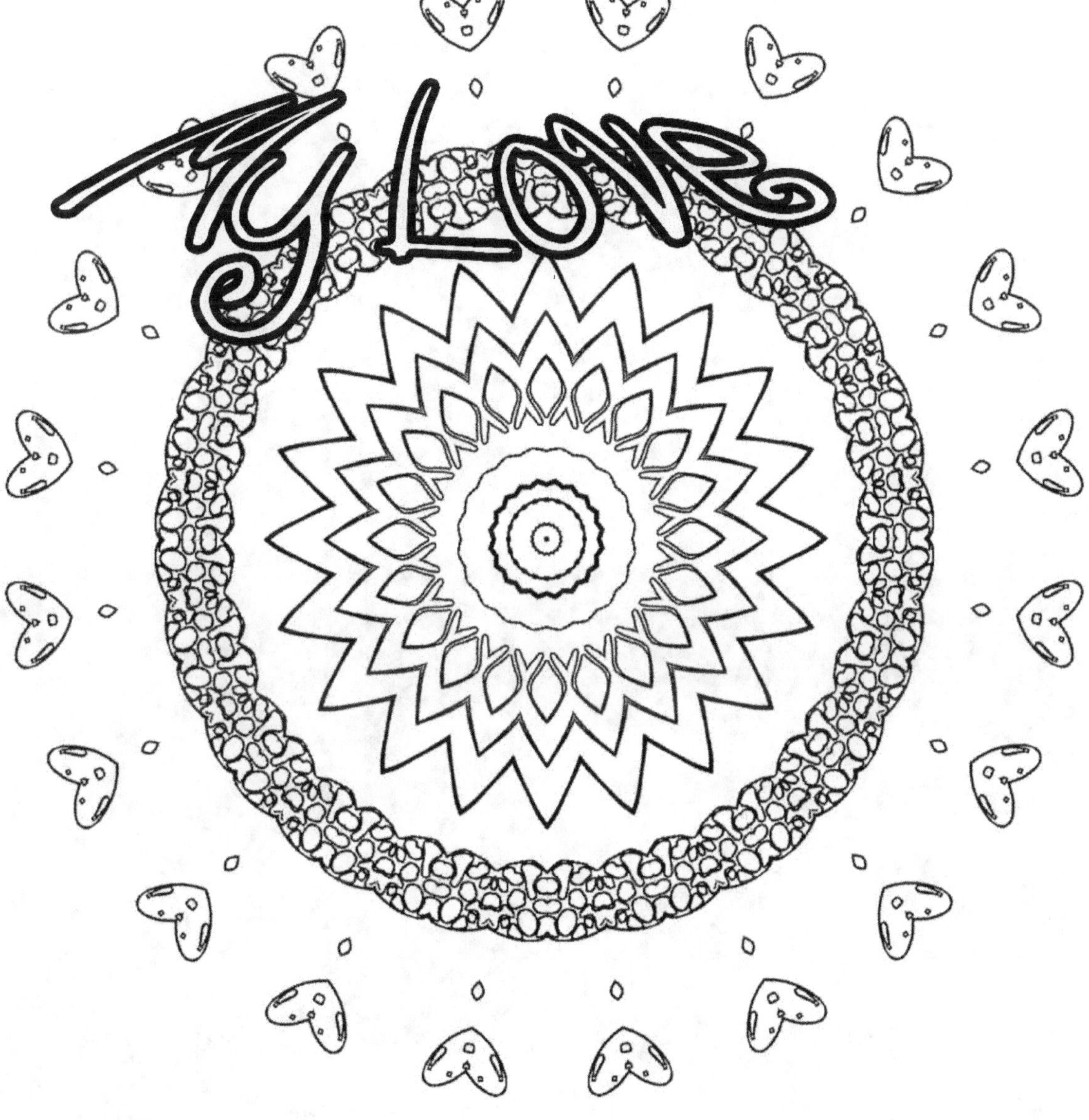
My Love

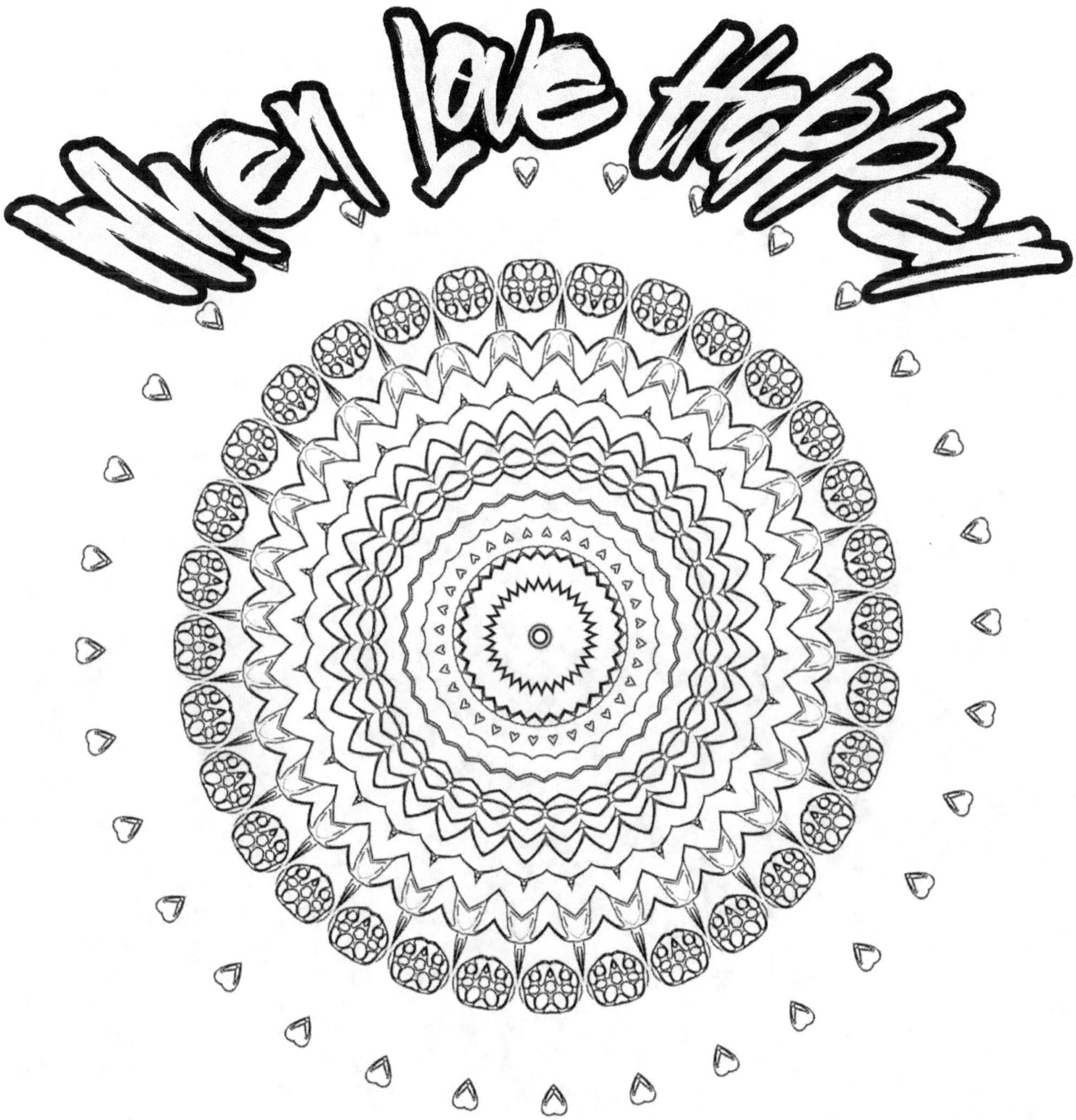
When Love Happen

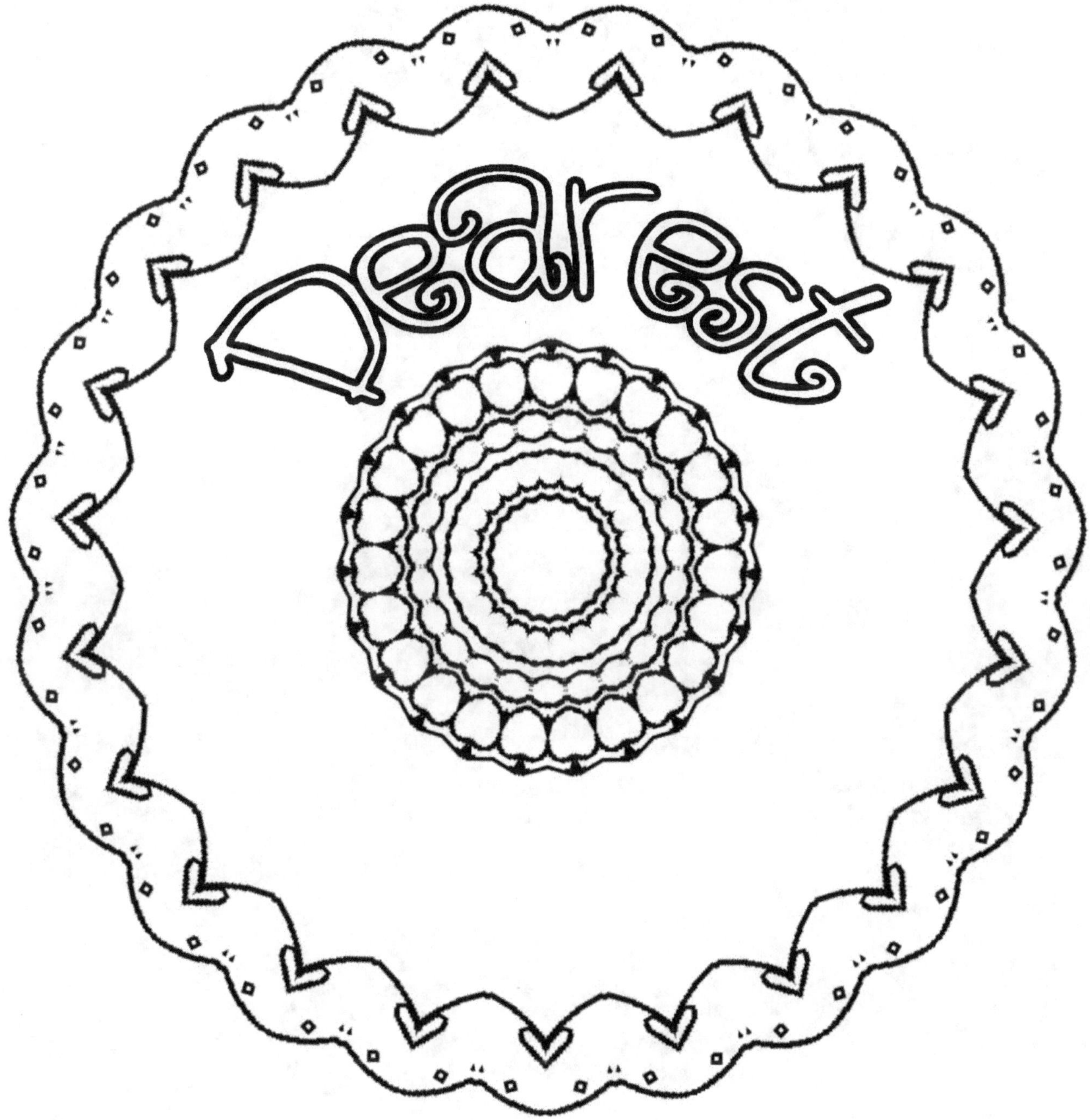
Dearest

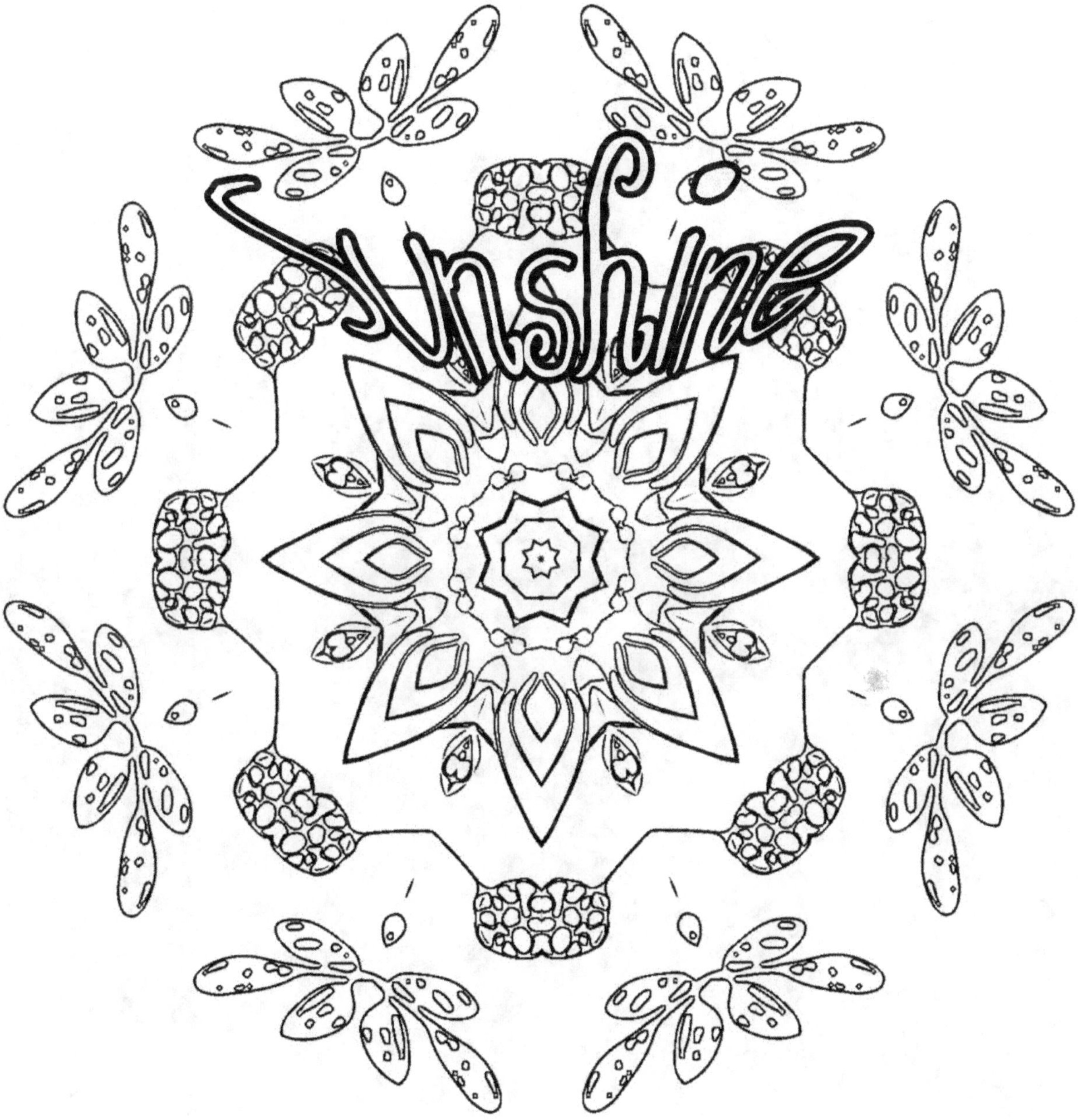
Sunshine

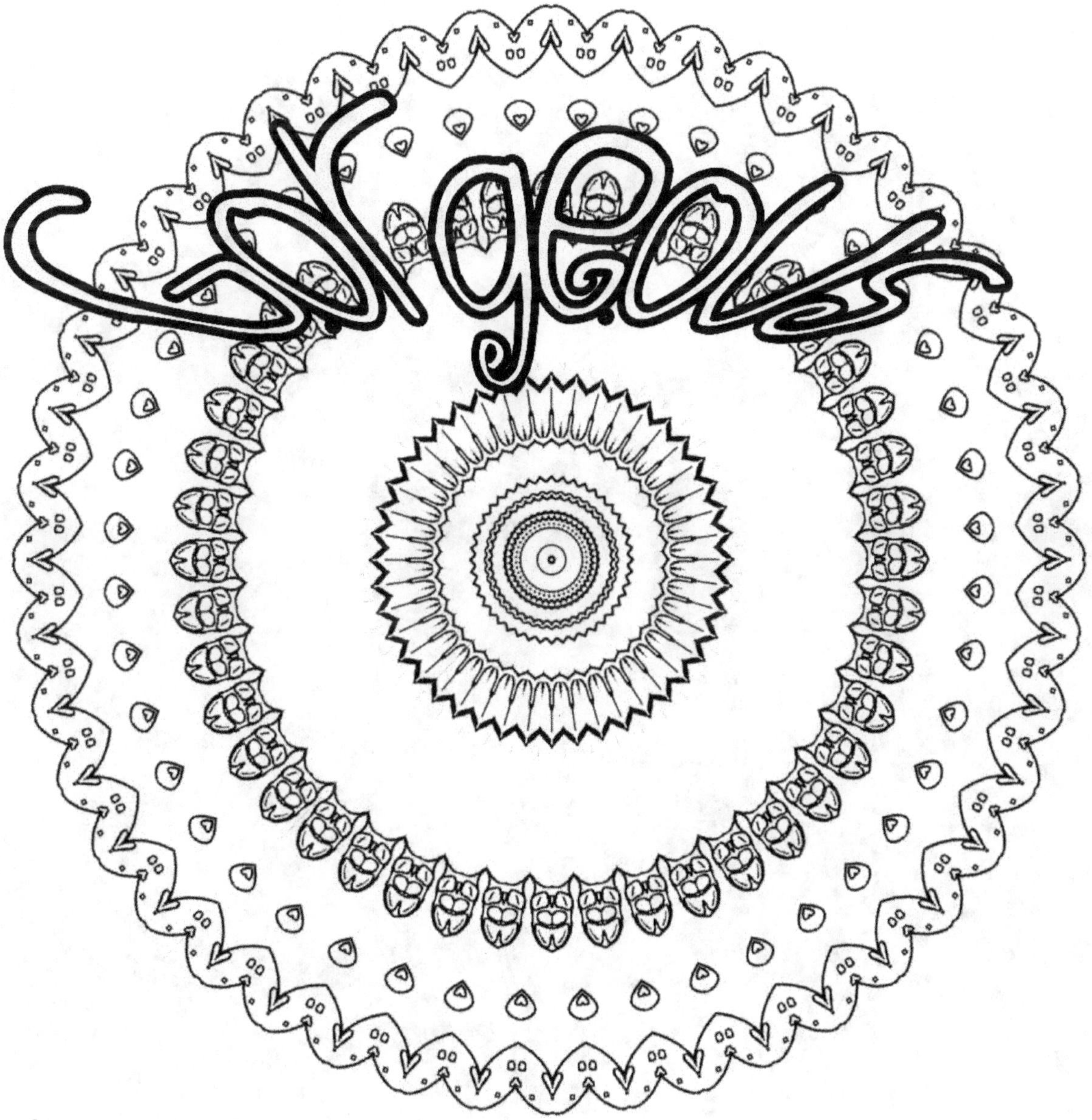